Hungry Planet

≋ Anna Claybourne ≋

W
FRANKLIN WATTS
LONDON • SYDNEY

Franklin Watts
First published in Great Britain in 2025 by Hodder and Stoughton
Copyright © Hodder and Stoughton Limited 2025

All rights reserved.

Editors: Amy Pimperton & Julia Bird
Designer: Rocket Design (East Anglia) Ltd

Alamy: Xinhua 28t.
Shutterstock: Viktoriia Ablohino 3tl, 40crb; Acrylic Vectors 17bl; Alfmaler 32tl, 32r, 33c; Amnise 42cr; Mubeen Arif 41br; Arif_Vector 11clb, 11crb, 11bla, 11bl; Art Me CD 30bl; Art n Peaches 32br, 48 crb; Artsholic 4br; AVA Bitter front cover cb; Baibaz 40b; Daria Balayeva 35tr; Beta757 31tr; Andrii Bezvershenko 11cr, 11bc; Bibadash 3tr, 23bl; Kristina Bilous 37b; Bits and Splits 7b; Xavier Boulenger 26bl; Bragapictures 12c; Joe Dordo Brnobic 24c; CamRosPhotography 33br; Catandchild 40tl, 40tr, 41t, 41tc, 41cl, 41cr; Chemkya 37cl, 41crb, 48c; Olga Chernyak 11c; Lexi Claus 23br; Colorfuel Studio 36c; Cosmaa 16cl, 16br, 41tc; Andy Dean Photography 28br; Demkadel 37tr; Doasan-graphic 11br; Oleksandr Drypsiak 4tl, 4br; Ekaterina Efstathiadi 4cr, 8t; Everett Collection 18bcl; Daria Falcon 21br, 47t; Fdant85 43c; Fevziie 9br; Flags Stock 10crb; Flex889 34tl, 34cb, 37trb; Fresh Vector 6t, 38bra; Flash Vector 9bl, 9bc, 38tl, 38tr, 38trc, 38br, 39tr, 39trb, 39crl, 39cr, 39bcb; Frogella 21cra; Good Studio 3bl, 4tr, 4tlb, 4l, 5cl, 5bc, 5br, 13tl, 13tr, 13c, 15tr, 15c, 15cr, 21crb, 29cl, 30t, 41clb; DronG 33cr; Graphic toons 34cl, 37tlb; GreenSkyStudio 12tr, 32clb, 48tlb; Grinbox 2; Guitar Photographer 35b; Tany Gust 22b, 27, 26–27b, 27c; Gvardgraph 10b; Hennadi 23crb; Illusionix 30c, 30cr; Ivector 3br, 9bcl, 9bc, 14r, 19tcr, 41bl; Nigel Jarvis 19bl; Juliasuena 35tc; Judy Jump cover b/g; Ilonka K-Art 27t; Dimitrios Karamitros 35cr; Kasman vector 10cra; Khlung Center 42bl; Luka Kikina 17c; Kikujiarm 5bl; King Vector 26c, 47b; Holger Kirk 17t; Tomasz Klejdysz 38bl; Yevgen Kravchenko f cover c; Jim Lambert 15bl; LamDong Agriscape 18c; Lemono b cover c, 4cr, 21tl, 39cl; Mian Lily 40cl; Limpreom 32bcl, 48clb; Look_Studio 37cr; Longjourneys 25b; Lusya Lukina 5cr; Ivan Bruno de M 8b; Macrovector 11cl; maggie.ri 39bc; Magr80 23cr; Manovector 14tl, 48tr; MarbleDesign 33tr; Riccardo Mayer 23t; Mentalmind 27br, 29cr, 41c, 45; MicroOne 13tc; Ulyana Mo 32crb, 48cr; Mosa Meat 34b; MugiMulya 21bl; Hamied Munandar 31cl; Nature line 42–43; Net Vector 29tl; No44ka 31crb; Nordroden 33cl; Alena Nv 29cr; Panaiotidi 21cl; Paper Trident 32cla, 33bl, 43b; PawLoveArt 15tcr; Ricky Adita Perdana 40crb; Perori 12tl, 12bl, 13br; Peipeiro 22c; PetiteARTist 6blc; Pikovit 14c; Tata Pikulina 18t, 18bl, 19tc, 19tr; Ergun_Pinar 36cr; Pixfinity Studio 34c; PlutusART 35cl; MikhailPopov 30–31b, 48b; Pressmaster 31br; Pretty Vectors 39br; Oleg Prokopenko 16c, 16cr, 16bl, 16bc; Promo_G 19tl; Heena Rajput 39tcb; Rhyzhkov Photography 10l; Richorzo 42l; Elena Rolau 22t; Alexander Ryabintsev 40c; Inna Sakun 38cl; Sensvector 14b, 15b; Onica Alexandru Sergiu 13bc; 7COLORSbd 20b, 21bc; Siberian Art 12cb, 12br, 38cr, 47c; Natali Snailcat 24-24bg; Somkiat Sriboonsong 6bl, 6bc, 6br; Olga Strelnikova 4cl, 46; StockSmartStart 7c; Sunnydream 11crb; Superheang168 11tr; Svend77 7cb; Aichurek Talgartbek 31cr; Viktor Tanaslichuk 9t; Tanyabosyk 31tl; The Maldivian Doctor 24t; S Thom 7tr, 19cl; Toyting 43t; Uiliaaa 15tc; Aleksandra Yaskova 29bl; Vector Map 18br; Vedpku 10cr; Visual Generation 29tr; Vladimmus 17br; Rumka vodki 23clb; Artsem Vysotski 10tr; adam_wasinowski 35trb; WeirdyTales 40cr; WhiteJack 24bl; WinWin artlab 7tc; WinWinFolly 32cl, 32cr, 37tl, 48tlc; Brian Woolman 20t; Shabana Yousaf 33bc; DI YU 32bl, 33t, 36b; Yulia_988 16t; Kirill_Z 15br.
Wikimedia: John Jabez Edwin Mayall, 1861, PD, 19cr; Russell Watkins/DFID,CCA 2.0 generic, 28bl.

Every effort has been made to clear copyright. Should there be any inadvertent omission, please apply to the publisher for rectification.

978 1 4451 9049 5 (hbk)
978 1 4451 9051 8 (pbk)
978 1 4451 9050 1 (Ebook)

Printed in Dubai

Franklin Watts
An imprint of
Hachette Children's Group
Part of Hodder and Stoughton
Carmelite House
50 Victoria Embankment
London EC4Y 0DZ

An Hachette UK Company
www.hachette.co.uk
www.Hachettechildrens.co.uk

All facts and statistics were correct at the time of going to press.

The authorised representative in the EEA is
Hachette Ireland, 8 Castlecourt Centre, Dublin 15, D15 XTP3, Ireland (email: info@hbgi.ie)

Contents

Everyone needs to eat!........4

Why we need food............6

Where food comes from 8

CASE STUDY
Rice 10

The journey of food 12

Food and health 14

Food shortages 16

CASE STUDY
The Irish Potato Famine......18

Food and the environment..20

Food and climate change ...22

CASE STUDY
Shark overfishing 24

What's the answer?..........26

Food and farm aid 28

Changing farming............30

Changing what we eat 32

CASE STUDY
Lab burgers....................34

GM foods 36

Reducing waste 38

What can you do?............40

The future of food............42

Glossary 44

Further reading 46

Index...........................48

Everyone needs to eat!

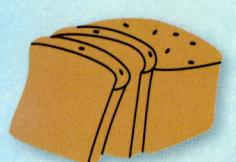

Everyone in the world needs to eat food to stay alive. To be healthy, we need to eat a range of different foods, and to get enough food each day. However, not everyone has this.

FOOD UNFAIRNESS

In many parts of the world, there's a reliable food supply, and most people can get enough to eat. Some people even have too much food, so some of it gets wasted.

Meanwhile in other parts of the world, some people struggle to get the food they need. There can be many reasons for this, including poverty, wars, government actions, or crops failing due to disease, pests, bad weather or natural disasters.

PLENTY OF FOOD

POVERTY AND HUNGER

A changing world

Governments, charities and international organisations, like the United Nations (UN), are trying to change things so that everyone has enough to eat. But our planet is facing challenges too. As the human population grows, and climate change affects farming and food supplies, it could become more difficult than ever to feed the world.

Climate change (see pages 22–23) can cause both floods that swamp crops and droughts that dry crops out.

THE FACTS AT A GLANCE

THE WORLD POPULATION PASSED 8 BILLION IN 2022, AND COULD BE OVER **10 BILLION** BY 2060.

3 BILLION PEOPLE, NEARLY 40 PER CENT OF THE WORLD POPULATION DOESN'T HAVE A RELIABLE SUPPLY OF HEALTHY FOOD.

ABOUT **800 MILLION** PEOPLE, 10 PER CENT OF THE WORLD'S POPULATION, ARE NOT GETTING ENOUGH FOOD.

IT'S A HUMAN RIGHT!

The Universal Declaration of Human Rights, agreed by the UN in 1948, states that every human has a right to enough food.

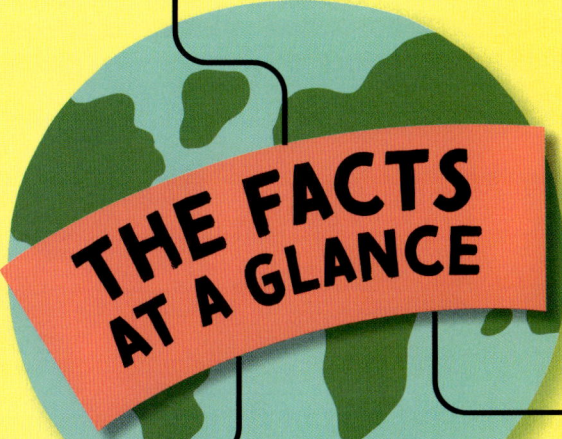

Can we fix it?

The world does actually produce enough food for everyone. We just need to find ways to share it out more equally, stop wasting it, and help people who are starving.

This book explores where food comes from, how farming and fishing affect the environment, why famines and food shortages happen – and what we can do to make sure everyone has the food they need.

New farming methods could help us to grow more food.

Why we need food

Have you ever wondered why you eat? Our bodies and brains tell us when we're hungry and need food. But why do we need it in the first place?

Staying alive

All living things need nutrients, or food chemicals, to do two main jobs. One is to grow and repair parts of the body, and to make new cells (the tiny parts that living things are made of). The other job is to provide the energy that cells and body parts need so that they can work.

Humans are animals, and animals have evolved to get food by eating. When we eat, our bodies break the food down into different nutrients, and use it for different jobs.

A SLICE OF PIZZA CONTAINS:

CARBOHYDRATES
Carbohydrates provide energy to power cells.

PROTEIN
Protein builds new cells, repairs damage and helps you grow.

FAT (E.G. IN OIL AND CHEESE)
Fat provides energy and helps the brain to work.

MINERALS AND VITAMINS (E.G. IN VEGETABLES)
These help particular body parts to work. For example, blood cells need iron to help them carry oxygen.

Plants don't eat like animals do, as they've evolved in a different way. They take in sunlight and use the light energy to convert water and carbon dioxide gas into food. This process is called photosynthesis.

CALORIES

Calories are a measure of how much energy food contains. We all need a certain amount of energy each day to keep our body working. The amount you need depends on things like your age and how active you are. For example, a child around the age of 9–12 needs about 2,000 calories a day.

Some foods contain a lot more calories than others.

CHEDDAR CHEESE:
403 calories per 100g

CUCUMBER:
15 calories per 100g

Changing over time

When humans first evolved, about two million years ago, we hunted and gathered food in the wild. But around 12,000 years ago, people gradually began farming. Keeping animals and growing crops made it easier to control our food supply, and helped the population grow.

Today, some food still comes from the wild, but most of it comes from farms. Many modern farms are huge, hi-tech operations, working vast areas of land.

A huge combine harvester cutting a wheat crop

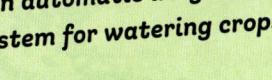

An automatic irrigation system for watering crops

Where food comes from

When you buy food from a supermarket, shop or cafe, you probably don't think too much about how it got there. But everything you eat has been grown and harvested, caught or collected by someone, somewhere.

What are we eating?

This pie chart shows how much of each type of food the world eats and where it comes from. In total, humans eat about 2.7 billion tonnes of food per year. That's an average of just over 300 kg per person per year (including babies and children).

About 25 per cent of our food comes from livestock farming, or keeping animals. It includes meat, eggs and dairy products including milk, yoghurt and cheese.

Less than 1 per cent is fish and other seafood, such as prawns, squid and mussels.

Over 70 per cent of our food comes from crop farming, or growing plants. That includes fruit, vegetables, nuts and seeds, and cereal crops such as wheat and rice.

And less than 1 per cent is wild food from hunting and gathering – foods such as wild mushrooms, nuts and berries, seaweed and wild animals that people hunt or trap.

In southern Africa, some people collect healthy, vitamin-filled wild fruits from uapaca trees to supplement their diet.

FARMING THE WORLD

Since farming began thousands of years ago, we've taken over more and more of the world's land for growing food. Today, about 40 per cent of Earth's land surface is used as farmland.

The world has over 500 million farms. They range from small subsistence farms where families grow food to feed themselves, to huge modern farms that can be bigger than a small country!

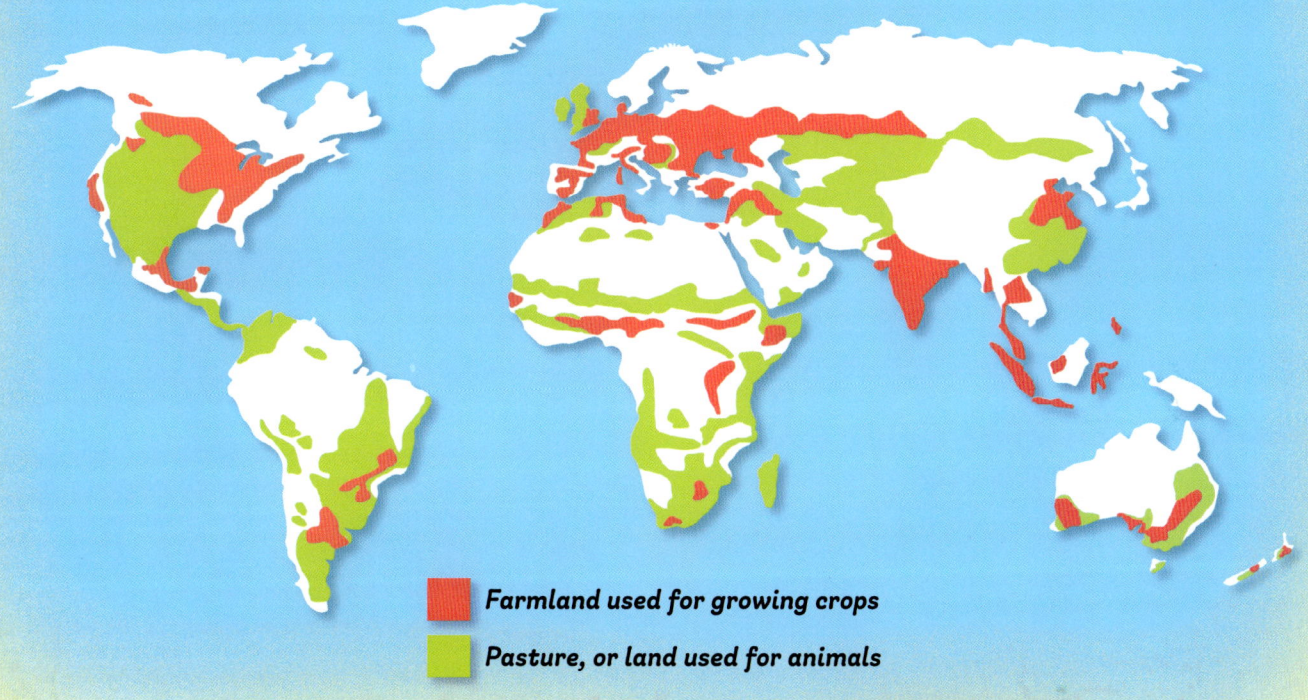

■ *Farmland used for growing crops*
■ *Pasture, or land used for animals*

Food waste

Amazingly, around 1.3 billion tonnes of food is wasted every year. So although we eat approximately 2.7 billion tonnes, we actually grow closer to 4 billion. Food waste can happen if crops get damaged or stored for too long, or while food is being transported. In shops and restaurants, food can sometimes go bad before being used or sold.

THAT'S NOT FOOD!

Not all farming is for food. Farmers also keep sheep and goats for their wool, and grow crops like cotton and linen for making fabrics, as well as other crops like flowers and medicines.

A crop of rose petals for making perfume oil

CASE STUDY

Rice

Have you eaten rice recently? Most people probably have! It's the most popular food on Earth, and is grown all around the world.

The five countries that produce the most rice are:

- CHINA
- INDIA
- INDONESIA
- VIETNAM
- THAILAND

Staple crops

Rice is a staple food, meaning that lots of people rely on it as a major part of their diet. Staple foods are often grains, as they're high in energy and easy to grow and store. Just three main grain crops – wheat, rice and corn (also called maize) – provide more than half of the energy that humans get from food.

Growing rice

Rice grows mainly in warm, humid parts of the world, and most types of rice need a lot of water. Farmers usually plant the crop in flooded fields called paddy fields.

A paddy field

Good value

Like other crops, rice can be affected by pests and diseases that can harm the plants. But it has a high yield, meaning you get a lot of food from each hectare (100 x 100 m area) planted. It's also high in energy and contains several important vitamins and minerals, so it's a very healthy staple food.

After harvesting, farmers separate the rice grains from the stalk and dry them, so they can be transported and stored.

RICE PRODUCTS

- Puffed rice cereal
- Rice wine
- Edible rice paper
- Rice milk
- Rice wine vinegar
- Sushi
- Rice flour
- Rice crackers
- Rice noodles
- Mochi, a Japanese rice paste snack

VERSATILE RICE
Rice is eaten boiled and sometimes fried, and can be made into all kinds of food and drink.

FACT FILE

★ LATIN NAME: Oryza sativa
★ LAND AREA: 165 million hectares
★ GLOBAL CONSUMPTION: 520 million tonnes per year
★ NUMBER OF VARIETIES: 40,000

The journey of food

Unless you pick a fruit off a tree and eat it straight away, all the food you eat goes on a journey to get to you, called the food supply chain. For most foods, the chain has several stages, and sometimes involves long distances.

FARMING OR PRODUCTION

The first step in the chain is production, or the farmer growing the food. These sunflowers are grown for their seeds, which will be used to make sunflower oil.

HARVESTING

When the sunflower crops are ready, the farmer harvests them. A machine separates the seeds out and loads them into a truck or trailer.

The seeds are transported to the processing plant.

PROCESSING

Processing means doing things to the food to make it ready to sell. Some foods are just washed, sorted and packed into boxes. Others go through more processing – like grinding wheat into flour, or pressing seeds to extract the oil.

Sunflower seeds have to be cleaned, de-hulled (have the tough seed covering removed), cooked and pressed.

Then the sunflower oil is put into bottles and labelled.

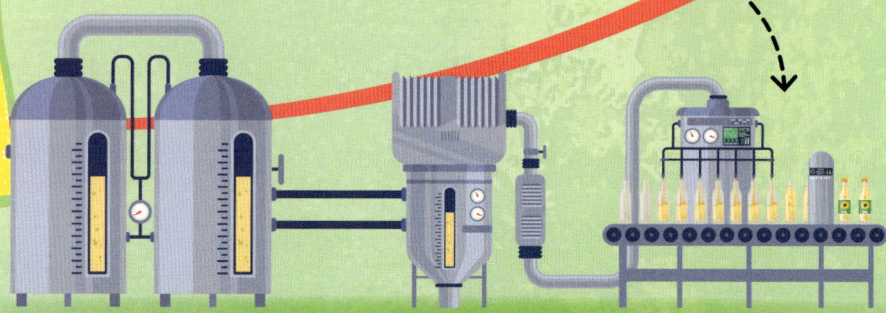

DISTRIBUTION CENTRE

At the distribution centre, food is stored in big warehouses. Supermarkets, restaurants or factories order the food they need, and it's collected and sent out to them.

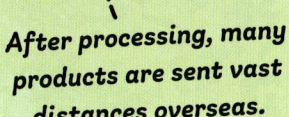

After processing, many products are sent vast distances overseas.

RETAIL

Retail is where the food is sold to consumers – the people who will use it. That could mean a supermarket, smaller shop, market stall, cafe or restaurant.

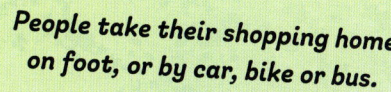

People take their shopping home on foot, or by car, bike or bus.

CONSUMPTION

The last stage is consumption, which means eating or using the food. For example, you could use sunflower oil to fry an egg, or to make salad dressing.

Problems on the way

Food supply chains like this bring us fresh, safe food from all over the world. But the longer a chain is, the more there is that can go wrong ...

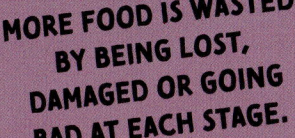

MORE FOOD IS WASTED BY BEING LOST, DAMAGED OR GOING BAD AT EACH STAGE.

TRANSPORTING THE FOOD FURTHER USES UP ENERGY AND CAN CAUSE POLLUTION.

LONGER JOURNEYS ARE MORE LIKELY TO BE DISRUPTED BY BAD WEATHER OR BREAKDOWNS.

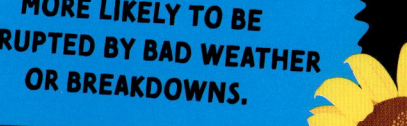

Food and health

To be healthy, we need the right amount of food, and the right kinds of food. If we don't have both of these, it can lead to poor health or disease.

Too much food

In prehistoric times, food wasn't always easy to find, so humans evolved to fill up on food when they could. Surplus (extra) calories from food turn into fat that gets stored in our bodies. Then, when food is scarce, the stored fat can provide energy.

Today, though, many societies have plenty of food, including high-calorie foods, and it can be easy to eat too much of them.

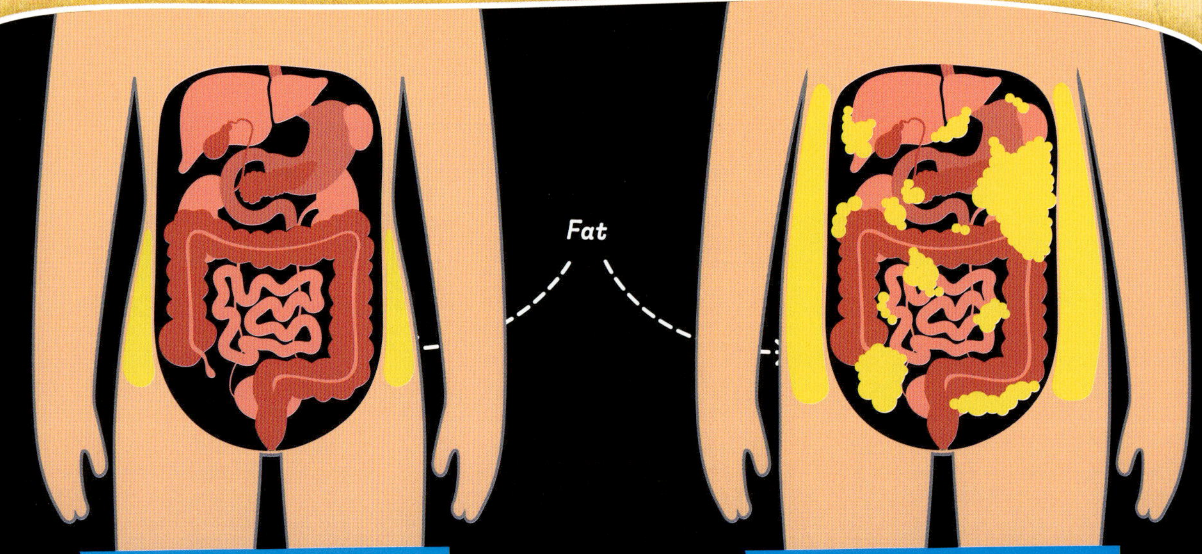

HEALTHY FAT

We need some fat in our bodies. Besides storing energy, it keeps us warm, cushions our organs and bones, helps the brain to work and enables the body to take in vitamins.

TOO MUCH FAT

But too much body fat can cause illness. It increases the risk of diseases such as diabetes, cancer, and heart and joint diseases.

Unhealthy food

In the modern world, there's a lot of highly processed food that contains additives such as food dyes and preservatives, or too much unhealthy fat, salt or sugar. These include things like factory-made cakes and cookies, fizzy drinks and fried fast food and snacks.

Fresher, simpler food is much better for us, but manufacturers make highly processed foods because they are cheaper, longer-lasting and taste good – so people will buy them. They contribute to health problems around the world.

HIGHLY PROCESSED FOODS LIKE HOT DOGS AND SUGARY CEREALS TASTE GREAT BUT THEY ARE UNHEALTHY.

(They are also called ultra processed foods.)

MALNUTRITION

Malnutrition means 'bad nutrition', and means you're not getting all the healthy nutrients you need. It can happen in both rich and poor countries, and can affect people even if they have plenty to eat.

For example, if you just ate lots of pasta and cheese, you'd get enough calories and energy, but no vitamin C, which is found in fresh vegetables, and fruits such as limes. A shortage of vitamin C causes an illness called scurvy, which leaves you tired and weak and can make your teeth fall out.

Long ago, many sailors got scurvy on long sea journeys, when they had to survive on stored dry food, such as hardtack biscuits.

Food shortages

Even worse than unhealthy food is not enough food, or no food at all. Throughout history, millions of people have died from starvation – and it's still happening.

Not enough food

We need food to live, so having no food at all is deadly, usually within a few weeks or months. However, even people who survive a food shortage or famine can still be badly affected.

A LACK OF FOOD CAN CAUSE:

Dizziness, tiredness, weakness and pain, making it hard to do work

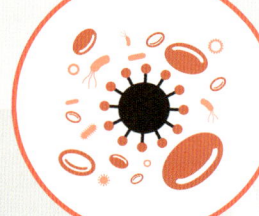

A weakened immune system (the body system that fights germs and diseases) – so people who are starving are more likely to catch diseases and infections

Problems with concentrating and sleeping

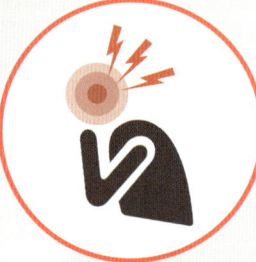

Stress, fear, anger and mental health problems.

A famine is a severe, long-lasting food shortage that leads to large numbers of people suffering malnutrition or starvation.

What causes hunger?

If there is enough food for everyone in the world, why does anyone go hungry? It can happen for various reasons, usually in poorer areas, remote places or countries at war.

★ FARMING PROBLEMS

Crops can fail or die because of droughts, being eaten by pests or damage by storms. Farm animals sometimes die from disease or food and water shortages.

★ NATURAL DISASTERS

A big tsunami, volcanic eruption, flood or earthquake can destroy farmland and food stores.

★ POVERTY

There may be enough food around, but some people can't afford to buy it. This can happen in very poor countries or countries with extreme inequality.

In some parts of the world, swarms of insects called locusts devour huge areas of crops.

Ash that erupts from volcanoes can destroy crops.

⇒ FOOD AND FIGHTING ⇐

One of the biggest causes of hunger around the world is conflict. During a war, people are often forced to leave their homes for safety, or are busy fighting, so they can't farm their land. Governments spend their money on weapons, so there's less for food, and fighting makes it harder for outsiders to get emergency aid to starving people.

HUNGER CAN LEAD TO EVEN MORE WAR IF PEOPLE START FIGHTING OVER SCARCE FOOD SUPPLIES.

CASE STUDY

The Irish Potato Famine

One of the most famous famines in history was the Great Famine, or Irish Potato Famine, which took place in Ireland from 1845 to 1852.

What happened?

The famine started when a plant disease called potato blight began infecting Irish potato crops. It turned newly harvested potatoes into a rotten, slimy mess that couldn't be eaten.

Many Irish people, especially in the south and west, were tenant farmers – meaning they didn't own their own land, but rented it. They survived mainly on the potatoes they grew. So when the crops failed, they soon began to starve. Witnesses described whole families looking like skeletons, and thousands of dead victims being buried in the fields.

Potatoes affected with blight

In just a few years, around a million people died from starvation and disease, and over a million more left Ireland, mostly going to the USA, to start a new life. Ireland lost a quarter of its population of around 8 million.

MAP OF IRELAND

Darker colour shows areas worst affected by the famine, where over 20 per cent of people died

An old illustration of starving farm workers during the Great Famine

DIGGING DEEPER

Potato blight was not the only reason that so many people starved. Blight infections caused food shortages in several parts of Europe, but they didn't all have famines. In fact, like many famines throughout history, this one had several causes. Politics, poor leadership, prejudice and other factors all played a part.

Irish tenant farmers were already very poor before the famine, so disaster quickly took hold.

They mainly used just one potato variety, the Irish Lumper. It grew well in Irish soil, but was at risk from disease.

GET OFF MY LAND!

At that time, Ireland was ruled by Britain, and rich English landowners owned a lot of the land. When Irish farmers couldn't pay their rent, they just threw them off the land, so they couldn't make a living.

FAMINE!

Meanwhile, other food from Ireland that could have been given to the potato farmers was exported to Britain instead.

British leaders, such as Prime Minister, Lord John Russell, failed to help the Irish people enough, maybe because they were far away or because they were seen as less important. Some did arrange aid schemes, but it wasn't enough.

A memorial to famine victims in Dublin, Ireland's capital

FACT FILE

★ DATES: 1845–1852

★ CAUSED BY: Potato blight, caused by the fungus Phytophthora infestans

★ DEATH TOLL: About 1 million

19

Food and the environment

Growing enough food for humans has a big impact on Earth's environment and landscape, as well as the many other species of living things that we share our planet with.

Land takeover

Farmers have always taken over wild, natural land to farm on. This isn't always a problem – for example, grazing goats on a mountainside doesn't stop other species from living there. But some farms change the landscape a lot more. For example, cutting down a forest and replacing it with a single crop destroys the habitat of thousands of wild plants and animals. It reduces biodiversity (the variety of different species), endangers wildlife and uses up the nutrients in the soil.

THE MONARCH BUTTERFLY

The monarch butterfly is now an endangered species due to losing large areas of its forest habitat. Farmers also use weedkillers to destroy the monarch's most important food plant, milkweed, as it can be poisonous for cows.

Conflict with wildlife

Since farming began, farmers have battled with wild animals feeding on their crops, or hunting their farm animals. It's not surprising, since farms take over wild animals' habitats. But when farmers shoot, trap or poison animals that threaten their crops or livestock, it can endanger or even wipe out wild species.

Wolves have disappeared from many parts of the world because of hunting by farmers.

Hunting and fishing

We still take food from the wild by hunting and fishing, and that can cause problems, too. Overfishing means fishing a species so much that it can't reproduce enough to replace its population, endangering fish or shellfish species (see pages 24–25). The same can happen with hunting wild animals for food.

The passenger pigeon died out after being hunted for food all over North America in the 1800s.

IN THE LAST 12,000 YEARS, EARTH HAS LOST AROUND ONE THIRD OF ITS FORESTS.

POLLUTION

Some farming and fishing methods release a lot of pollution into the environment. It can come from:

Smoke and gases being released from burning crop stalks, or from farm machinery engines.

Pesticides and weedkillers sprayed onto crops, harming wild plants and animals. These chemicals can also cause 'runoff' pollution when rain washes them into rivers.

Plastic waste, such as discarded fishing nets or plastic sheeting for covering crops.

21

Food and climate change

The world is getting warmer, and its weather patterns are changing, because of pollution in the air. Farming and the food industry help to cause climate change, and are affected by it too.

How it works

Earth's atmosphere – the layer of air around the planet – contains small amounts of greenhouse gases, including methane and carbon dioxide. They trap the Sun's heat like a greenhouse, helping to keep the world warm.

SUN

Heat from the Sun

Greenhouse gases trap a lot of the Sun's heat.

EARTH

Earth's atmosphere

The amount of greenhouse gases in the air is now increasing – especially carbon dioxide – which is released when we burn fuel. This causes rising temperatures, or global warming. It affects the weather in different ways, depending on where you are in the world.

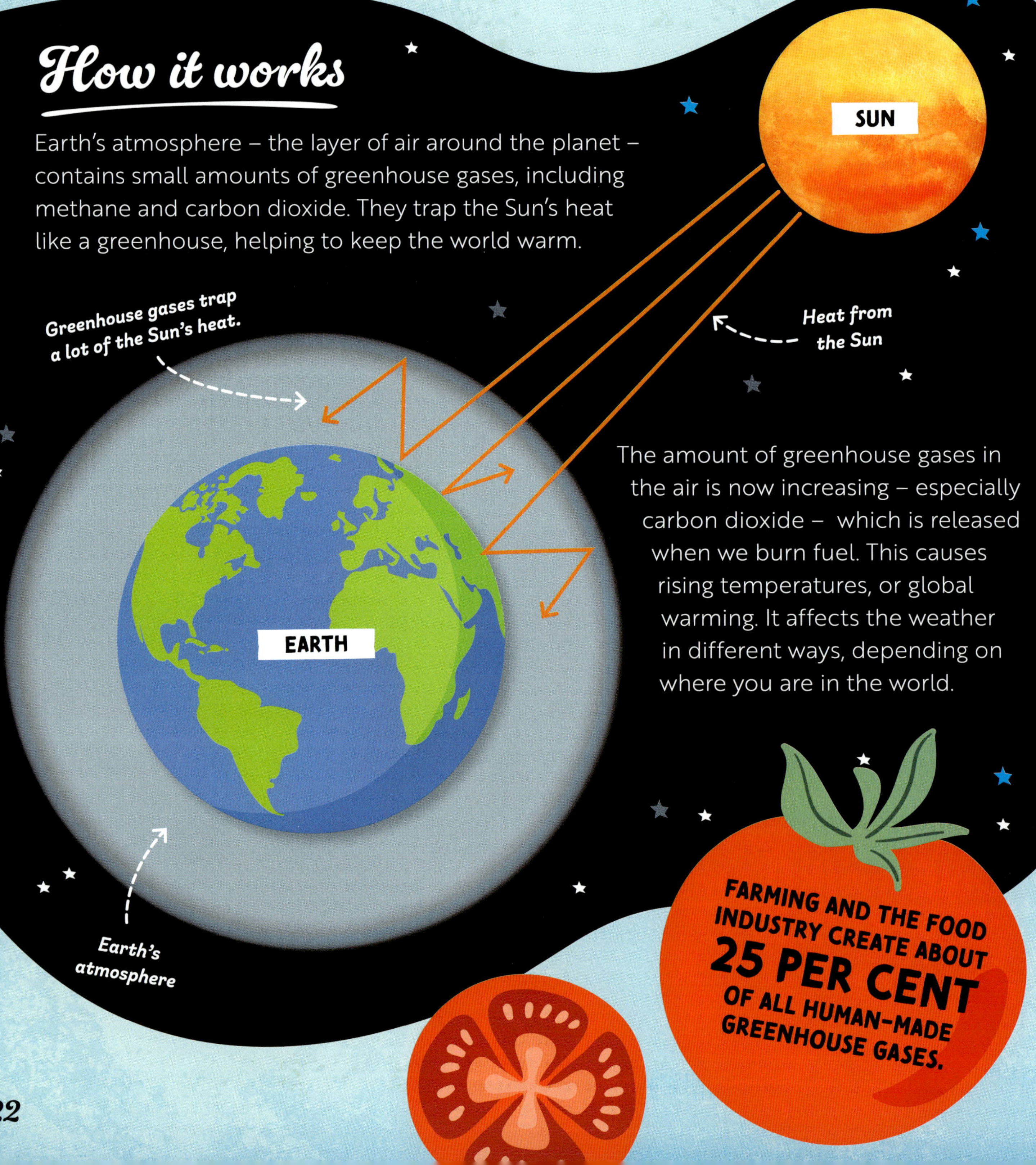

FARMING AND THE FOOD INDUSTRY CREATE ABOUT 25 PER CENT OF ALL HUMAN-MADE GREENHOUSE GASES.

The threats to farming

Farming relies on the weather, so climate change is causing a lot of problems for farmers.

★ More heat makes more water evaporate from the sea, causing bigger, more powerful storms, especially near coasts. They can flatten or flood farmers' fields.

★ In some areas, climate change is causing more droughts and hot, dry weather. This causes water shortages, and sometimes wildfires that destroy farms.

★ As the world warms, polar ice and glaciers are melting and flowing into the sea, making the sea level rise. When salty seawater floods the land, it contaminates the soil, and animals' drinking water.

Climate change is causing drier weather and droughts in the Sahel, an area of Africa just south of the Sahara Desert.

THE THREATS FROM FARMING

Farm vehicles, food processing plants and food transport all use fuel and release carbon dioxide.

Fertilisers used on farms release another greenhouse gas: nitrous oxide.

UNFORTUNATELY, GROWING AND TRANSPORTING FOOD ALSO CONTRIBUTES TO CLIMATE CHANGE.

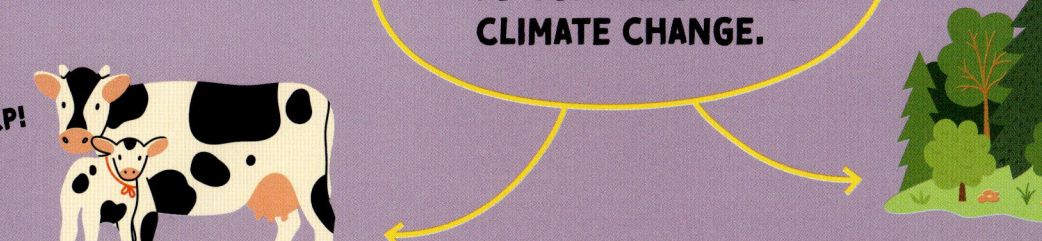

BURP!

Some farm animals release a lot of methane – a powerful greenhouse gas – as they digest food.

Forests take in a lot of carbon dioxide from the air, as plants use it to make food. So cutting down forests to make farmland contributes to climate change, too.

CASE STUDY

Shark overfishing

About a third of the wild fish species caught for food are overfished. That means too many are being caught, so their populations fall and cannot recover. This is especially bad news for sharks.

Sharks as food

Sharks are famous for eating humans, but we eat a lot more of them than they do of us! Shark attacks are actually very rare, but humans kill over 100 million sharks a year for food – ranging from small sharks like the spiny dogfish, to bigger species such as the scalloped hammerhead.

The scalloped hammerhead is one of the many overfished shark species.

SHARK FINNING

Millions of sharks are killed just for their fins, which are used to make traditional shark fin soup. Often fishermen just cut the fins off and throw the rest of the shark back into the sea, where it dies.

Shark fin soup is made from the strands of cartilage found inside the fins.

DISAPPEARING SHARKS

Overfishing affects sharks especially badly because most sharks are slow-growing species. Fish that have a short life cycle and lay hundreds of eggs can replace their numbers quite quickly, even if lots of them get caught. But sharks take an average of ten years to reach adulthood and start having babies (called pups), and don't have many babies at once. So, if a shark species is overfished and its population falls, it takes a very long time to recover.

THE WORLD POPULATION OF OCEAN SHARKS, AND THEIR RELATIVES, RAYS, HAS FALLEN BY AROUND **70 PER CENT** SINCE 1970.

Success stories

Governments, fishing organisations and charities are trying to make changes to protect sharks, and for some species it's starting to work. For example, several countries have now banned shark finning and shark fin soup, and some species are protected by laws that restrict how many can be caught.

The oceanic blacktip shark population fell sharply in the 1980s and '90s because of overfishing, but restrictions on catching it mean the population is now rising again.

FACT FILE
SHARK FISHING

★ NUMBER OF SHARKS CAUGHT PER YEAR: Over 100 million

★ NUMBER OF SHARK SPECIES: About 500

★ NUMBER OF SPECIES ENDANGERED: About 170, 1/3 of all species

What's the answer?

The human need for food has had a disastrous impact on our planet's forests and wild species. Yet many millions of people are still hungry. How can we make sure everyone has enough food, and help the planet too?

Sustainable changes

The food production industry is currently 'unsustainable' – meaning it can't carry on as it is without causing more damage and running out of land, water or other supplies. So the world is trying to make it sustainable instead.

1 ENDING HUNGER

The UN has set a 'Zero Hunger' target to end hunger and malnutrition by the year 2030. As well as delivering food to people who urgently need it, this also involves working with governments and charities around the world to help people to grow more food, and reducing poverty so that everyone can afford enough to eat.

The UN is an international organisation made up of most of the world's countries, working together to try to solve hunger, conflict and other global problems.

2 NEW (AND OLD) FARMING METHODS

We're inventing new farming methods that require less space, fertiliser and other chemicals. At the same time, some farmers are returning to old traditional methods that can make farming easier and more sustainable.

In Africa's dry Sahel region, farmers have revived the traditional zaï crop farming method, planting crops in small pits in the soil that trap scarce water.

3 DIFFERENT FOODS

Some foods use up more land or cause more pollution than others, so changing our diets can help. Scientists are also developing new foods that can be made in other ways.

Eating more plant foods and less meat saves farmland, as meat takes much more space to produce.

4 REDUCING POLLUTION

To fight pollution and global warming, we need more farm machinery and food processing plants that use renewable electricity instead of fuel. Transporting food shorter distances can help, too.

5 REDUCING WASTE

Everyone at every stage of the food supply chain can reduce food waste by using better storage methods and systems for sharing out surplus food.

Food and farm aid

At the moment, millions of people are going hungry, so the most urgent change is to make sure everyone has enough food right now.

Vital support

Food aid is food – or sometimes money to buy food – that's delivered to people who desperately need it. It might only be for a short time in an emergency, like a flood or earthquake. Or it might go on for longer, for example during a long drought or war.

Governments can give food aid to poor people in their own countries. But countries around the world also donate money and food to help hungry people in the poorest places. The UN has an agency called the World Food Programme that works to organise and deliver the aid.

Workers prepare food aid to be distributed to people in Kabul, Afghanistan.

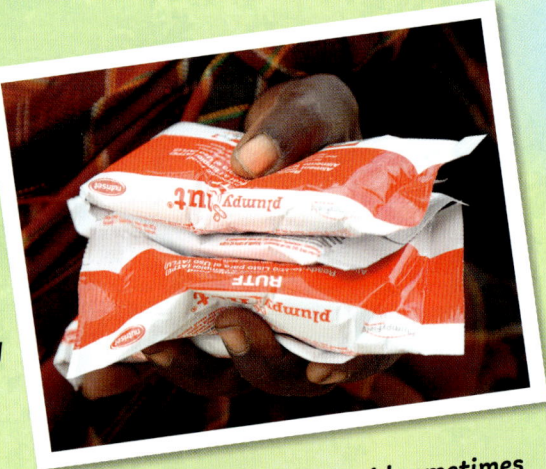

As well as everyday foods, aid sometimes includes sachets of high-energy, high-protein food that's easy to eat and doesn't need cooking, as a treatment for malnutrition.

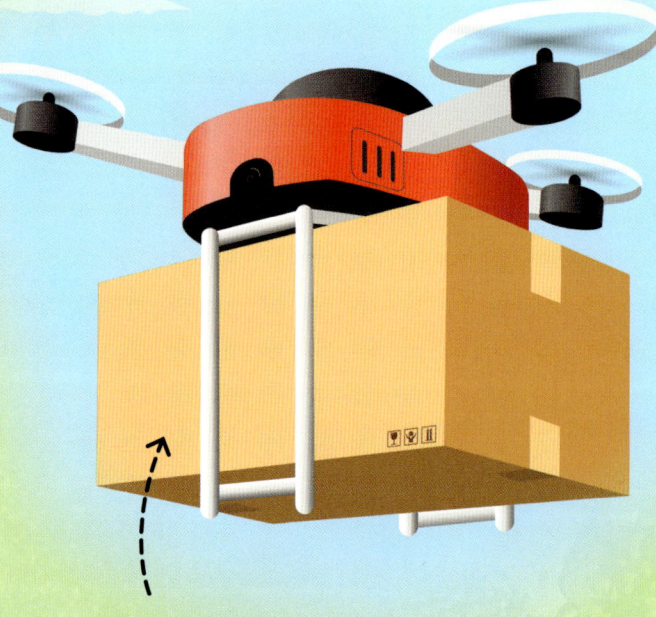

Technology, such as drones and hi-tech airships, can help to deliver aid to remote places, or areas where roads are cut off by wars or disasters.

★ NEW CROPS

New varieties of crop can be developed to suit a drier climate or produce a bigger yield. They help farmers to make a better living.

★ MONEY

Grants, subsidies or loans let farmers buy the seeds, animals, machinery or land they need.

★ FAIR TRADE

Fair trade schemes have been set up to pay farmers a fair price for the food they grow, so that they can survive and compete with bigger businesses.

HELP FOR FARMERS

Instead of needing food aid, it's better if people can grow their own food, or sell what they've grown to make a living. So helping farmers is a good way to prevent hunger, too.

★ HEALTHIER LIVESTOCK

Vaccinations and medicines for livestock save farmers from losing their animals to illness.

★ INTERNET

Internet connections help farmers to find useful information and advice, share machinery and sell their products online.

29

Changing farming

Can we grow food sustainably, without harming the environment so much, or taking up so much space? Farmers are finding inventive ways to do this.

REGENERATIVE FARMING

Regenerative farming is becoming more and more popular. It combines traditional and modern farming methods to try to improve the soil and environment and make them healthier, instead of damaging them. As the soil is richer, this results in better yields and healthier crops and animals. Regenerative farming methods include:

★ Not ploughing or disturbing the soil, to protect its natural ecosystem. Instead, crop stalks and weeds can be left to cover the soil, then rot back into it, adding more nutrients.

SOIL SCIENCE

Soil is incredibly important for farming. It contains bacteria, fungi and tiny animals that fill it with nutrients and help plants to grow. Pesticides, weedkillers and monocultures (growing just one crop species) can wear soil out, kill some soil organisms and use up nutrients. Regenerative farming reverses this by keeping the soil as healthy as possible.

★ Switching land between growing different types of crop and grazing animals, so that the soil nutrients can recover and stay in balance.

★ Recycling waste plant parts into compost, and using compost and animal manure (poo) as fertiliser, instead of artificial fertilisers that can cause pollution.

★ Combining grazing land with orchards or woodland, and using hedgerows full of plant species and animal habitats instead of walls or fences. This encourages biodiversity, and also adds more nutrients to the soil.

★ Landscaping fields so that rain naturally flows across and waters them.

★ Some regenerative farmers also farm organically, meaning they don't use any artificial chemicals.

Vertical farming

Vertical farming means growing smaller crops in trays, stacked on top of each other on shelves, inside a greenhouse or other building. It saves space, and protects crops from pests, weeds and weather. And you can control the lighting and temperature, so it works all year round. Though vertical farming does use energy, it can be eco-friendly if the energy comes from renewable sources such as wind or solar power.

VERTICAL FARMING MAKES IT EASIER TO GROW CROPS IN A SMALL AREA, INCLUDING IN CITIES AND HOMES — SO IT CAN ALSO REDUCE THE DISTANCES THAT FOODS NEED TO BE TRANSPORTED.

Vertical farming works well for many food crops, including salad leaves, potatoes, strawberries and tomatoes.

Changing what we eat

We can also help the environment, and still grow enough food for everyone, by switching to foods that use up less farmland, water and energy. That means eating less meat and more plants – but also eating other foods.

SWITCHING TO PLANTS

Why are plants better for the planet? It's because growing a crop of rice, potatoes, apples or other plant only takes one season or year. Farm animals usually take longer to grow – and on top of that, they have to be fed. So even more farmland is used for growing crops like corn and oats for farm animals to eat.

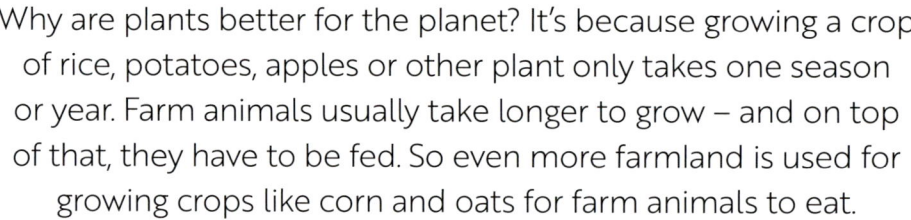

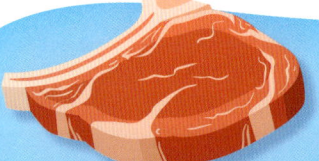

PRODUCING 1 KG OF RED MEAT, SUCH AS BEEF OR LAMB, USES OVER 300 M² OF LAND.

300 M²

3 M²

BUT GROWING 1 KG OF RICE, BANANAS OR POTATOES USES LESS THAN 3 M².

Eating less or no meat means we can grow much more food on less land. Even with a bigger world population, if everyone ate mostly plants, we could turn large areas of farmland back into natural forests and wilderness. Food would be cheaper too, as meat is usually more expensive than plant-based food.

As vegetarian and vegan diets become more popular, there are now lots of animal product alternatives available, like sausages made from beans, and milk alternatives made from soy beans, oats or rice.

New foods

We've also started to invent new foods made from things that aren't animals or plants, such as fungi and bacteria. Humans have always eaten mushrooms, but smaller types of fungi can be grown in big vats and used to make a meat alternative called mycoprotein. Scientists have also made a high-protein flour called Solein, grown from harmless bacteria that feeds on water and gases from the air, which can be made into many different types of food.

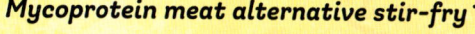

80% OF THE WORLD'S FARMLAND IS USED TO RAISE ANIMALS AND GROW ANIMAL FEED.

Mycoprotein meat alternative stir-fry

Mycoprotein is grown in industrial fermenters like these.

EATING INSECTS

Farming insects could be another way to grow healthy food without harming the planet. Many cultures around the world already eat various types of insect, including locusts, ants and caterpillars. They are high in protein, grow fast and don't need much space to farm.

Crackers made from cricket flour

CASE STUDY

Lab burgers

There are plenty of vegan and vegetarian burgers made of beans, vegetables and mushrooms. But what if you could make a burger out of real meat – without using animals? It's already happening!

MEAT FROM A LAB

To do this, scientists use a method called cellular agriculture. They take cells from animal muscle (which is where most meat comes from) and grow them in a nutrient-filled liquid. The cells naturally grow and divide in two to make more cells. As long as they have the right chemicals to feed on, which can come from plants, they will keep multiplying. That creates real meat, grown in a lab instead of a field.

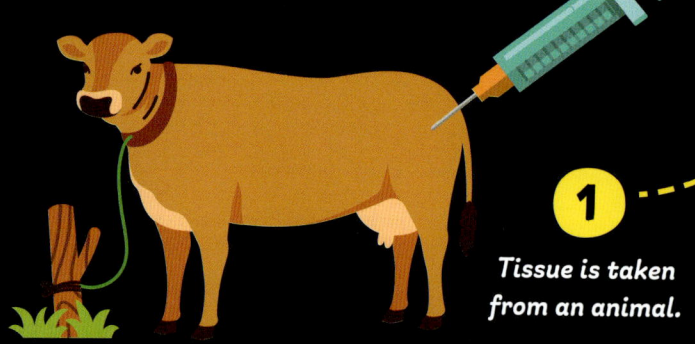

1 *Tissue is taken from an animal.*

6 *The cultured meat is ready to be consumed.*

The challenges

It's not quite as easy as that, though, because the meat's texture and shape is different from when it grows on an animal. It's easy to make burgers, but harder to make realistic fresh meat. Scientists are experimenting with structures called scaffolds for the meat to grow on, or using a kind of 3D printing to build up layers of meat cells.

Some labs have already created lab-grown burgers and other meat, and it's for sale in a few restaurants.

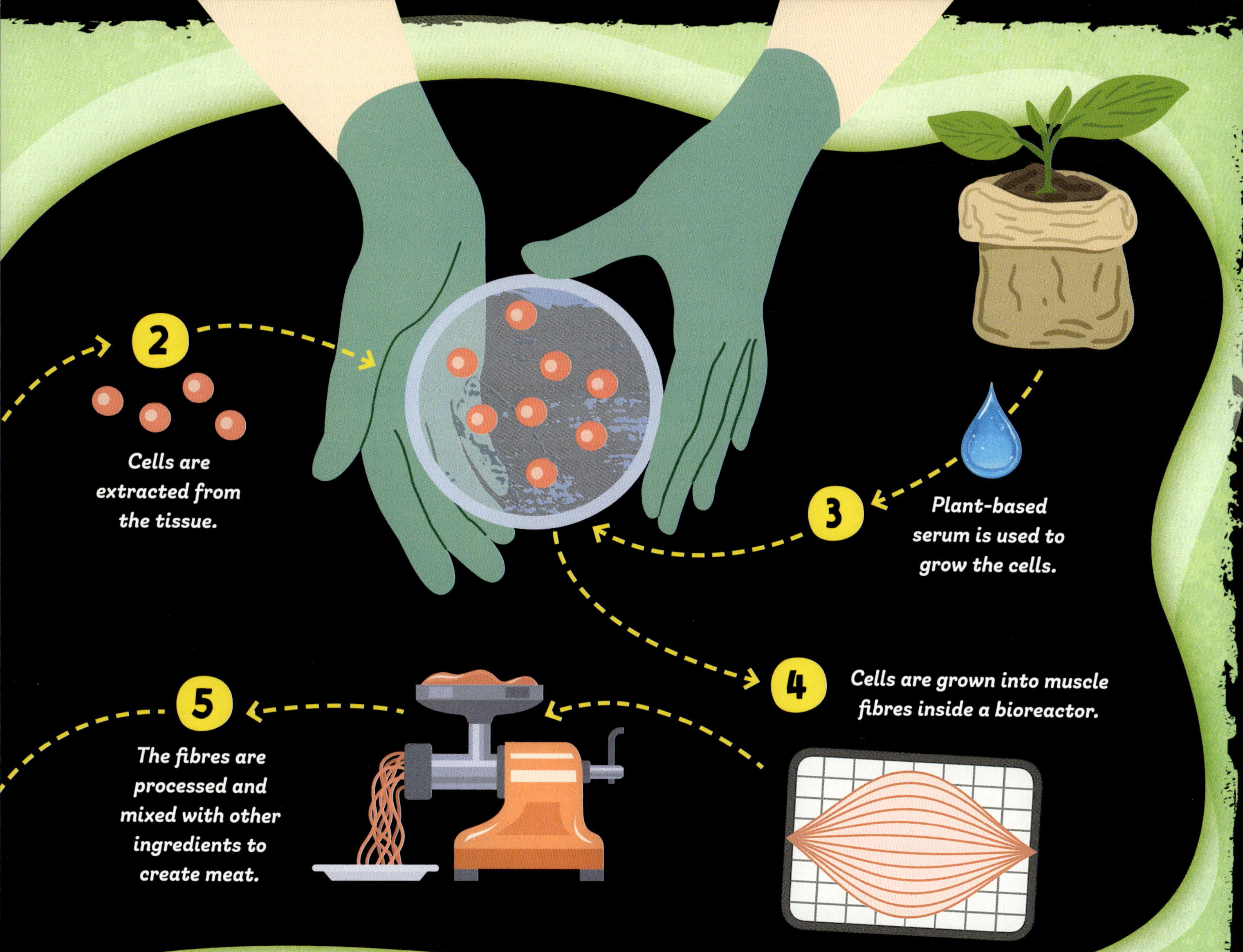

2 Cells are extracted from the tissue.

3 Plant-based serum is used to grow the cells.

4 Cells are grown into muscle fibres inside a bioreactor.

5 The fibres are processed and mixed with other ingredients to create meat.

Future food

If lab-grown meat takes off, it could change the food industry all over the world. We wouldn't need to use huge areas of land to raise and feed animals for meat. We could make meat anywhere, so we wouldn't have to transport it long distances. And we wouldn't kill billions of animals every year.

MORE ANIMAL PRODUCTS

Cellular agriculture could be used to make a wide range of animal products:

★ Meat such as lamb, pork, chicken, turkey and bacon

★ Fish and seafood

★ Milk and other dairy products like butter, yoghurt and cheese

★ Eggs

★ And maybe non-food animal products as well, such as wool, leather and silk.

Most countries have rules for looking after farm animals' welfare. But many are still kept in crowded, uncomfortable cages and have unhappy lives.

GM foods

GM is short for Genetically Modified, and it's another modern food invention. A GM food has had some of the DNA in its cells changed to make the plant or animal grow or work in a different way.

HOW IT WORKS

Living things are made of tiny cells. They contain genes – instructions that control how a living thing grows and works. Genes are made of a stringy substance called DNA (short for DeoxyriboNucleic Acid).

To make a GM crop, scientists take a useful gene from one living thing, and add it to a cell from another living thing. Then they let that cell grow and copy itself, making a plant or animal with the extra DNA in all its cells.

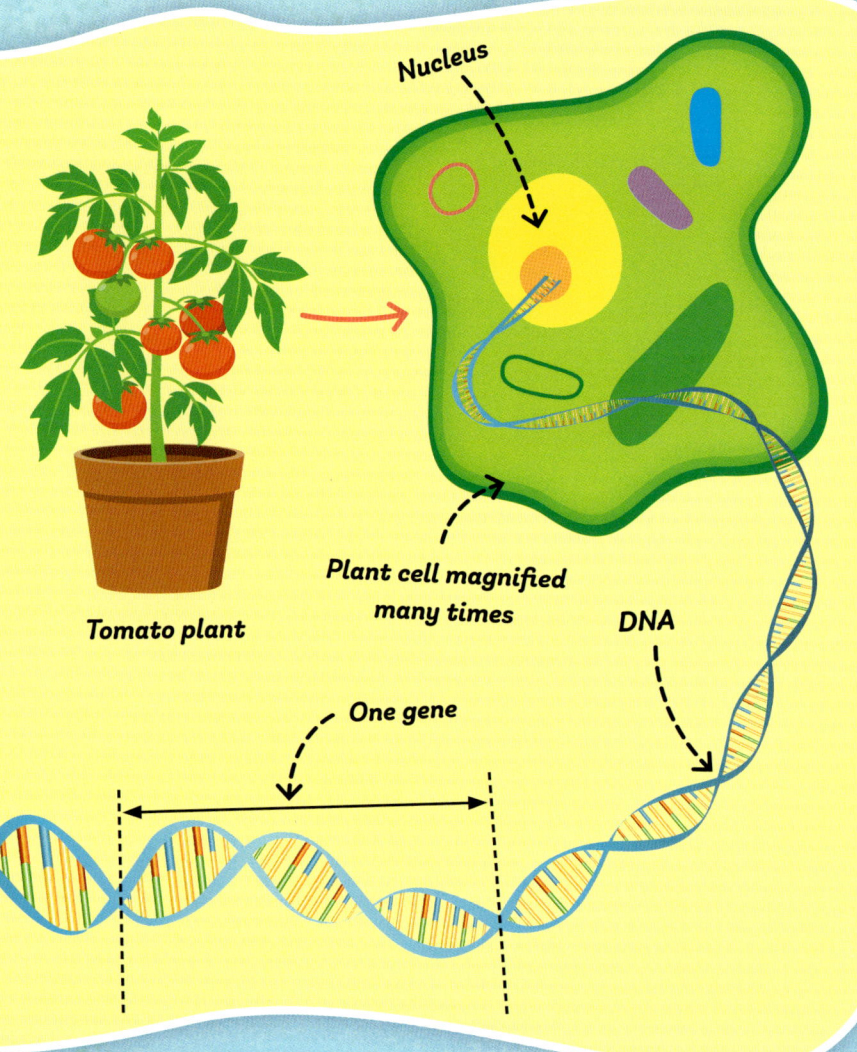

Tomato plant

Nucleus

Plant cell magnified many times

DNA

One gene

In practice

For example, if a bacterium species has a gene that makes a chemical that harms insects, scientists can remove that gene from the bacterium. Then, they insert that gene into the DNA of a tomato plant. The plant can now make the same chemical to make it poisonous to insects. The plant's seeds also now contain the extra gene, so more GM tomatoes can be grown.

Insects such as aphids can destroy plant crops.

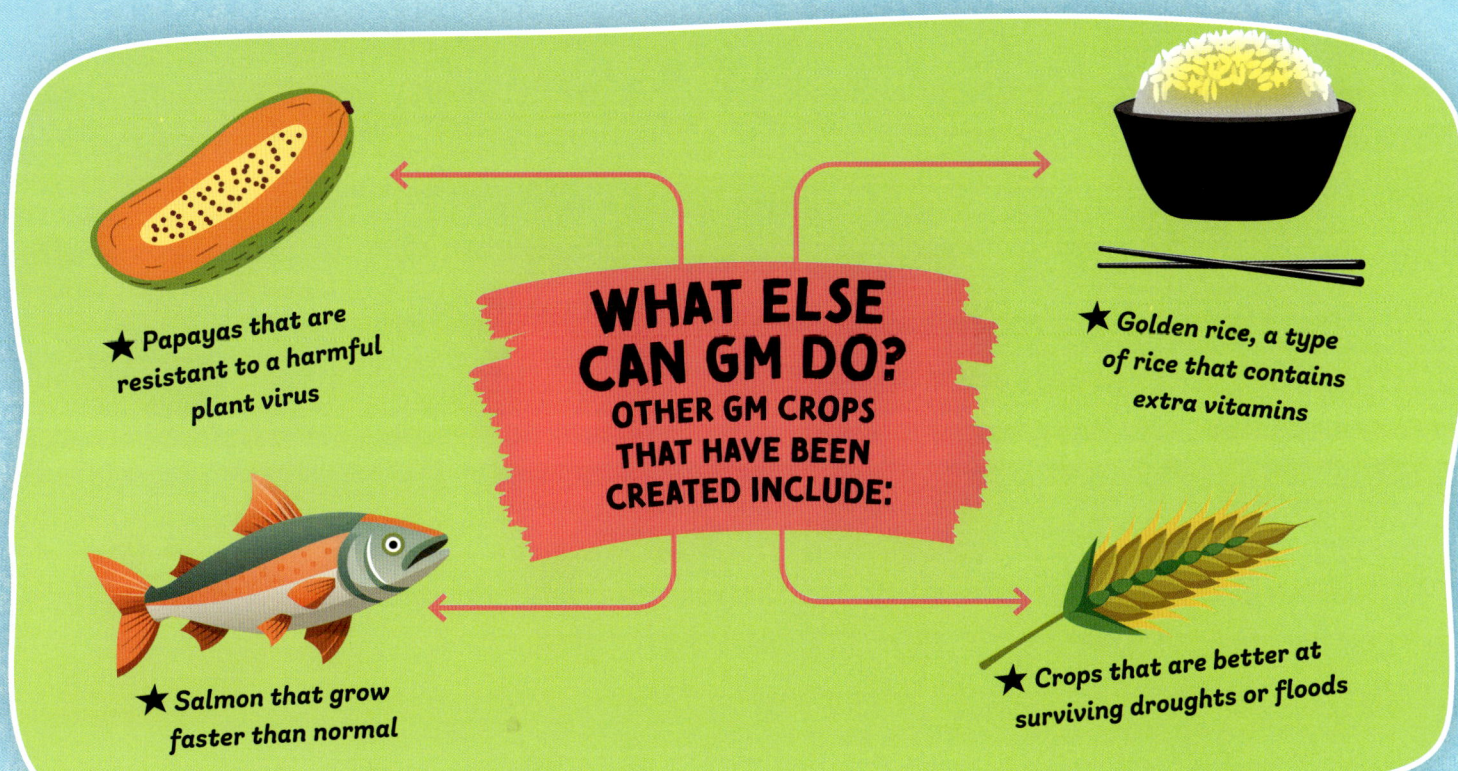

WHAT ELSE CAN GM DO?
OTHER GM CROPS THAT HAVE BEEN CREATED INCLUDE:

★ Papayas that are resistant to a harmful plant virus

★ Golden rice, a type of rice that contains extra vitamins

★ Salmon that grow faster than normal

★ Crops that are better at surviving droughts or floods

Pluses and minuses

GM crops can help to feed more people, and also help the environment. For example, using a pest-resistant GM crop means farmers can avoid using polluting pesticides. Drought-resistant crops can save water and cope with climate change.

But there can be problems, too. For example, insect-resistant crops are bad for wild insects, which reduces biodiversity. Some people worry that GM foods could be harmful for humans too, although they are carefully safety-tested.

TOP CROP
GM SOYBEANS ARE THE BIGGEST GM CROP IN THE WORLD, COVERING AN AREA OF ABOUT 90 MILLION HECTARES (THAT'S ABOUT THE SIZE OF NIGERIA).

Reducing waste

A whole THIRD of the food the world produces is wasted (see page 9). So if we could stop wasting it, it would be much easier to feed everyone in the world, both now and in the future.

Saving food at every stage

It's probably not possible to end all food waste, as some food will always go bad, be eaten by pests or get damaged while being transported. But we can reduce as much food waste as possible by making changes at every stage of the food supply chain.

ON THE FARM

★ Use leftover plant parts to make compost to use as fertiliser, or as food for animals.

★ Sell food in several different ways, for example to supermarkets, but also at a farmer's market or farm shop, or by delivering veg boxes, to use up surplus produce.

★ Vertical farming can protect against pests and weather.

★ Some GM crops can reduce damage from pests, frost, droughts or floods.

Farming black soldier fly larvae is a good way to use up food waste. The larvae feed on the waste, and can then be used to make food for farm animals and fish.

PROCESSING PLANTS

★ Find uses for trimmed-off or unused food parts – for example making them into pet food or compost.

★ Instead of throwing them away, use squashed or misshapen fruit and veg to make products like sauces or ready meals.

★ Produce a range of product sizes, so people don't have to buy more of something than they need.

Milk can be sold in different quantities to suit people's needs.

38

DISTRIBUTION CENTRES AND TRANSPORT

★ Use packaging that protects food from damage.

★ Longer-lasting GM food means less waste.

★ Reduce distances so food doesn't have to travel as far.

IN SHOPS AND SUPERMARKETS

★ Sell wonky fruit and veg and slightly damaged products at a discount instead of throwing them away.

★ Have a bargain shelf for food that's near its sell-by date.

★ Set up schemes to send unsold food to food banks or homeless shelters.

★ Give shoppers ideas and recipes to help people store or use up spare food.

Unsold food can be passed on instead of wasted.

YOU CAN REDUCE FOOD WASTE AT HOME, TOO. TURN OVER TO FIND OUT HOW.

39

What can you do?

How can you change the future of farming and help to feed the world? It might sound like a big task, but there is actually a lot each person can do, through the foods we choose to buy and eat, and in other ways.

Eat plants!

One of the biggest ways to help is to eat less meat. The more we replace meat with plant foods, the less space we need for farming. Not everyone wants to be vegetarian or vegan, but you could try having a few meat-free meals a week. How about ...

Pasta with tomato sauce, pesto or mixed veg

Bean burgers or vegetarian sausages

Chickpea or paneer curry

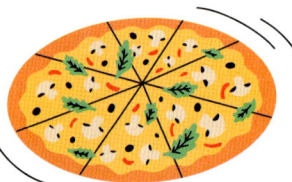
Veggie pizza – try topping with olives, spinach, red peppers or mushrooms

Tofu, vegetable and noodle soup

Cut the distance

Food often travels a long way to get to you, adding to emissions that cause global warming. To reduce this ...

★ Check where foods are from and choose the most local ones, if possible.

★ If you can, shop at farm shops or farmers' markets, which often sell food grown or made locally.

★ You could even try growing some food yourself at home!

You might be able to get a regular veg or food box delivery from a local farm.

LESS WASTE

THERE ARE LOTS OF WAYS TO REDUCE FOOD WASTE AT HOME TOO, AND WHEN YOU EAT OUT.

WHEN YOU'RE SHOPPING:

★ Only buy what you need, and stick to a shopping list.

★ Check the sell-by or use-by date and make sure you have time to use each item.

★ Don't buy extra food on special offer if you can't use it up.

★ Don't reject fruit and veg that's wonky or not perfect-looking!

AT HOME:

★ Freeze leftovers instead of binning them, if you can.

★ Check the dates on the foods you have to make sure you use them up in time.

★ If possible, put veg trimmings, eggshells and other food waste that can't be eaten into a food waste recycling bin. Or make a compost heap in your garden, if you have one.

EATING OUT:

★ Avoid ordering too much – you can always order something else if you're still hungry.

★ If you have leftovers, ask for a bag or box to take them home in.

LESS WASTED FOOD ALSO MEANS YOU SAVE MONEY – SO IT'S A GREAT HABIT TO GET INTO FOR WHEN YOU GROW UP.

The future of food

The ideas explored in this book are already starting to change food and farming around the world. But there could be even more hi-tech and sci-fi solutions in the future.

Eat wood!

Although we eat fruit and nuts from trees, we can't eat wood. It contains a lot of a tough material called cellulose that humans can't digest. Scientists are experimenting with using GM bacteria to turn wood into food. The bacteria feed on the wood and make edible carbohydrate chemicals. Another method uses a type of yeast that feeds on wood and grows, making a protein-rich food.

We don't want to cut down more trees, but this method could work on waste wood, such as sawdust, and on other plant parts we can't eat, like crop stalks, corn cobs and nut shells.

Termites can eat wood because they have a type of bacteria in their stomach that helps them to digest the cellulose.

High-protein flour can be made from yeast that feeds on wood.

ROBOT FARMING

Some farmers already use robots to help with picking fruit, planting seeds or spraying crops. As robots get more advanced and cheaper, they could take over more farming jobs.

★ Drones can survey farmland quickly from the air to spot weeds, flooding or pests.

★ Robot pickers can work constantly to harvest a crop before it goes bad.

★ In the future, whole vertical farms could be run by robots, providing food supplies wherever they're needed.

Tomatoes being harvested by a robot picker

SCI-FI SOLUTIONS

In some sci-fi shows, astronauts use food replicators that can assemble atoms and molecules into any kind of food, using nanotechnology (technology on a tiny scale) to recycle waste. In theory, this is possible. Nanotechnology is not advanced enough yet, and a replicator would use a lot of energy – but in the future we might be able to make any food using just a machine.

Can we do it?

Climate change, a growing population and news stories about famines can be scary – but don't panic! There is enough food for everyone, and we are already changing the way farming and the food supply chain work. Eventually, we should be able to make sure no one has to go hungry, and let more of the world return to its wild and natural state.

Glossary

Agriculture Another name for farming.

Atmosphere The layer of air around Earth.

Bacteria Very small, single-celled microorganisms, or tiny living things.

Biodiversity The variety of living things in a particular habitat, or in the whole world.

Blight A type of disease that affects plants, such as potatoes.

Calorie A unit of energy, used to measure the energy in food or fuel, or the energy used up by activities.

Carbon dioxide (or CO_2) A gas found in the air, produced as waste by animals when they breathe, and used by plants to make food.

Carbohydrates A type of nutrient found in food, which provides the body with energy.

Cells The tiny units that living things are made up of.

Cellular agriculture Growing foods such as meat from cells.

Cellulose A tough substance that forms the structure of most trees and other plants.

Climate The typical weather conditions in a particular place or area.

Climate change A long-term change in climate patterns.

Compost Rotted plants or leftover food, used for improving soil.

Consumer Someone who buys or uses food, or other things.

DNA (DeoxyriboNucleic Acid) A chemical found in cells, used to encode instructions that make the cell work.

Drought A period of very dry weather that can cause water shortages and harm crops.

Ecosystem A particular area or place and all the living things that are found there.

Endangered A living thing at risk of dying out and becoming extinct.

Environment The surroundings, especially natural surroundings or the natural world.

Evaporate To change from a liquid into a gas.

Evolution A process of gradual change over multiple generations of living things.

Fair trade Buying and selling food at a fair price that allows farmers to make a living.

Famine A long-lasting, widespread and severe food shortage that can cause starvation and death on a large scale.

Fat A type of nutrient found in food that provides energy and helps the brain to work.

Fertile Used to describe land or soil that is good for growing crops.

Fertilisers Chemicals or substances added to soil to make it more fertile.

Finning Catching sharks only for their fins, which are used to make soup.

Food aid Providing emergency food supplies, or money to buy food, to those who need it.

Food supply chain The sequence of farming, harvesting, processing, transporting and selling that food goes through on its way to the consumer.

Fungi A group of living things that includes mushrooms, moulds and yeast.

Genes Sequences of chemicals arranged along strands of DNA, which act as coded instructions for cells.

Glacier A large, slow-moving mass of ice on a mountain or in a polar area.

Global warming A gradual increase in Earth's average temperature over the last two centuries, caused by human activities.

GM foods Food from crops or animals that have had their genes altered, or modified, to make them grow better or produce more or better food.

Grant Money given to someone to help them start a business or produce something.

Graze To let farm animals feed on grass or other outdoor plants.

Greenhouse gases Gases that contribute to the greenhouse effect, such as carbon dioxide and methane.

Habitat The natural home or surroundings of a living thing.

Harvest To cut and gather a crop so that it can be used as food.

Immune system The body system that kills germs and fights diseases.

Irrigation Watering crops.

Larva A baby insect that has a different form from its parents, such as a caterpillar.

Livestock Farm animals.

Loan Money that is lent to a person or country.

Malnutrition A lack of the right kinds of food.

Manure Animal droppings or dung, especially when used as a fertiliser.

Methane A greenhouse gas that is released by farm animals such as cows.

Minerals Pure, natural, non-living substances, such as metals or salt. The body needs some types of mineral to help it work.

Nutrients Food chemicals that do useful jobs in the body.

Organic farming Farming without using artificial fertilisers, pesticides or other chemicals.

Overfishing Catching too many fish, so that fish populations cannot recover and start to fall.

Paddy field A flooded field used for growing rice.

Pasture Grasslands or meadows used for grazing animals.

Pesticide A chemical used to kill pests, such as insects that eat crops.

Population Number of people.

Poverty The state of being very poor.

Prehistoric From the time before history was first written down.

Preservatives Chemicals added to food to stop it from going bad, so that it lasts longer.

Processing Preparing food to be sold, for example by cleaning it or cooking it.

Produce Products grown by farmers, such as fruit and vegetables.

Protein A type of nutrient found in food that helps the body to grow and repair damage.

Regenerative agriculture A type of farming that focuses on keeping the soil healthy, avoiding pollution and supporting biodiversity.

Renewable energy Energy from sources that don't run out, such as wind, waves and sunshine.

Run-off Chemicals used in farming that get washed out of the soil into rivers, causing pollution.

Reproduce To breed or have babies.

Scurvy A disease caused by a shortage in the body of vitamin C.

Species The scientific name for a particular type of living thing.

Staple food A food that makes up a large part or the main part of your diet.

Subsidy Money given to farmers to help them make a living.

Subsistence farming Growing food to feed yourself and your family.

Sustainable Able to be continued in the same way over a long time.

Unsustainable Unable to continue in the same way over a long time.

Vegan Someone who doesn't eat or use any animal products.

Vegetarian Someone who doesn't eat meat.

Vertical farming Growing crop plants indoors in trays, stacked up vertically.

Vitamins Chemicals or nutrients in food that the body needs in small amounts to stay healthy.

Wildfire A large, out-of-control fire in a forest, grassland or other wild area.

Yield The amount of food or other products that come from a farm or crop.

Zaï farming A farming method used in dry climates, involving growing crops in small pits dug to catch water.

Further reading

BOOKS

100 Things to Know About Food
By Sam Baer, Rachel Firth, Rose Hall, Alice James, Jerome Martin, Parko Polo and Federico Mariani (Usborne Publishing, 2017)
A round-up of food facts, figures and interesting information.

101 Small Ways to Change the World
By Aubre Andrus (Lonely Planet Kids, 2018)
Lots of fun, simple, practical ideas for making everyday changes to make the world more sustainable.

Guardians of the Planet: How to be an Eco-Hero
By Clive Gifford and Jonathan Woodward (Buster Books, 2019)
How to help the planet with a wide variety of activities, projects and everyday habits, from helping wildlife and cleaning up the coast to running a green home.

Stand Against: Poverty and Hunger
By Alice Harman (Franklin Watts, 2020)
An introduction to world poverty and hunger and how to campaign against it.

Take a Bite: Eat Your Way Around the World
By Aleksandra and Daniel Mizielinski (Big Picture Press, 2022)
Fun book exploring foods around the world and where different foods come from, including recipes to try.

The World That Feeds Us
By Nancy Castaldo and Ginnie Hsu (words & pictures, 2023)
Visit a variety of farms around the globe to discover what they grow and their different food-growing methods.

What Can We Do?: Poverty and Food
By Katie Dicker (Franklin Watts, 2024)
This book explores how poverty and hunger are linked, how its impact is felt around the world, and what can be done to combat it.

WEBSITES

kids.nationalgeographic.com/nature/save-the-earth
The National Geographic Kids Save the Earth website, with activities, quizzes and lots of information.

www.climatekids.org/food
The Climate Kids website's section on food systems is loaded with science experiments, activities and facts.

www.twinkl.co.uk/teaching-wiki/farm
The Twinkl website has a section on farming that explains what a farm is and includes lots of useful farming facts and words.

www.worldfoodmap.org/
Visit the World Food Map website and click on a country to find out about its favourite foods. The site also has useful facts about food groups and types.

WATCH

www.bbc.co.uk/newsround/59911562
Watch this CBBC *Newsround* video on practical ways we can reduce food waste.

www.youtube.com/watch?v=1bIsFIfz9_A
This YouTube video from EIT Food shows a day in the life of a UK farmer.

Note to parents and teachers: every effort has been made by the Publishers to ensure websites are suitable for children, that they are of the highest educational value, and that they contain no inappropriate or offensive material. However, because of the nature of the Internet, it is impossible to guarantee that the contents of these sites will not be altered. We strongly advise that Internet access is supervised by a responsible adult.

Index

Africa 8, 23, 26, 37
animals 7, 8, 9, 17, 20, 21, 23, 24-25, 26, 29, 30, 32, 33, 34, 35, 36, 38
Asia 10, 28

biodiversity 20, 31, 37

chemicals 6, 20, 21, 23, 26, 30, 31, 34, 36, 42
climate change 4, 22-23, 27, 37, 40, 43
crop diseases 4, 11, 18-19, 37
crop failure 4, 17, 18-19
crop pests 4, 11, 17, 31, 36, 37, 38
crops 4, 7, 8, 9, 10-11, 17, 18-19, 20, 21, 23, 26, 29, 30, 31, 32, 36, 37, 40, 42, 43
    cereal 7, 8, 10-11, 12, 15, 32
    fruit 8, 12, 15, 31, 32, 36, 37, 38, 39, 40, 41, 42, 43
    nuts 8, 42
    seeds 8, 12, 29, 36, 37, 40, 43
    staple 10, 11
    vegetables 6, 8, 15, 18-19, 31, 32, 34, 38, 39, 40, 41

dairy products 6, 8, 15, 32, 35, 38
deforestation 20, 21, 23, 42
diseases, human 14, 15, 16, 18

eggs 8, 13, 35, 41
Europe 18-19

fair trade 29
famine 5, 16, 17, 18-19, 43
    Irish Potato Famine 18-19
farming/farms 4, 5, 7, 8, 9, 10, 11, 12, 17, 18-19, 20, 21, 22, 23, 26, 27, 29, 32, 33, 38, 40, 42, 43
    organic 31
    sustainable 30-32
    technology 7, 29, 42, 43
    vertical 31, 43
fertiliser 23, 26, 31, 38
fish/fishing 5, 8, 21, 24-25, 35, 37, 38
    overfishing 21, 24-25
food aid 17, 19, 28-29, 39
food processing 12, 13, 15, 23, 27, 34-35, 38
food production 5, 10, 11, 12-13, 26, 27, 38
food shortages 4, 5, 16-19, 26, 28, 43
food supply 4, 5, 7, 8, 26
    food supply chains 12-13, 27, 38-39

food transportation 9, 11, 12-13, 23, 27, 28, 31, 35, 38, 39, 40
food waste 4, 9, 13, 27, 31, 38-39, 41
genetically modified (GM) foods 36-37, 38, 39, 42
governments 4, 17, 19, 25, 26, 28
growing food (see crops)

harvesting 7, 8, 11, 12, 18, 43
healthy foods 5, 8, 11, 14-15
hunting 7, 8, 20, 21

insects 17, 33, 36, 37, 38, 42

malnutrition 15, 16, 26, 28
meat 8, 15, 27, 32, 33, 34, 35, 40
    lab-grown meat 34-35

natural disasters 4, 17, 28
    droughts 4, 17, 23, 28, 37, 38
    floods 4, 17, 23, 28, 37, 38, 43
new foods 27, 29, 32, 33, 34-35
North America 18, 21
nutrients 6-7, 8, 11, 14-15, 20, 28, 30, 31, 33, 34, 37, 42

overeating 14

pesticides 21, 30, 37
plants 6, 8, 18, 20, 21, 23, 27, 31, 32, 35, 36, 40, 42
pollution 13, 21, 22, 27, 31, 37
population growth, human 4, 5, 7, 32
poverty 4, 17, 18-19, 26, 28

recycling 31, 41
rice 8, 10-11, 32, 37

shopping/shops 8, 9, 13, 38, 39, 41
starvation (see famine)

unhealthy foods 15
United Nations (UN) 4, 5, 26, 28

vegan foods 32, 34, 40
vegetarian foods 32, 34, 40

war 4, 17, 26, 28
water 6, 7, 10, 17, 23, 26, 31, 32, 33, 37
weather 4, 13, 17, 21, 22-23, 31, 38
wild foods 7, 8, 21, 24-25